How To Speak With Impact

Without Changing Your Personality

Andrew Lancaster

TABLE OF CONTENTS

<u>Conclusion</u>

Clear and impactful communication is the key to all interactions from personal chats to corporate negotiations. Whether you need to speak to a crowd, converse one-on-one, or send an email or text, you need to understand the underlying factors that make the contact work. Communicating with impact allows you to fully engage with the other people involved in the conversation. It facilitates the spread of important information while inspiring and motivating others to take the type of action most beneficial to the situation.

Some people are natural born communicators who fall back on innate charisma and loquacity to attract and keep attention. Others balk at the idea of taking responsibility for conveying important information or making a targeted impact with oral or written words. No matter where you fall on this spectrum, you can improve your ability to communicate with impact without changing your personality or putting on an 'expert orator' act.

These types of interaction may seem simple. After all, you have been talking and writing most of your life. However, mastering the art of making an impact and truly engaging with others requires full understanding of foundations, principles, and methods that contribute to forging connections.

Start with the basics. Identify the challenges. Learn to develop true mastery.

Communicating with impact is about more than getting the words out. It is about conveying understandable meaning, influencing others effectively, and paying just as much attention to your audience's needs and interests as your own.

A- Understanding Key Principles of Communication

Before you have a hope of improving your communication skills, you must understand the foundation principles that create an effective exchange of information. If someone asks you what communicating is, you might list methods like speaking, writing emails, and texting. These, however, are merely the vehicles that carry whatever you want to convey to another person or group.

Successful communication is about so much more than getting an idea out into the world in the general direction of your target audience or people engaged in a back-and-forth conversation.

1) What is Communication?

The Merriam-Webster dictionary defines communication as "a process by which information exchanged between individuals through a common system of symbols, signs, or behavior." The second definition, "personal rapport," is just as essential to understanding what communication is. If you do not have a rapport or connection with other people involved, you will not be able to exchange information effectively.

With Whom Do You Communicate?

Communication is often more than a two-way street. In business environments, messages and conversations may include a dozen people or more. Public speaking at a special event or convention may involve hundreds. Of course, this ability also affects personal relationships in a huge way.

Effective interactions depend partially on knowing the other people involved. You cannot simply speak or write and expect everyone to understand and accept it equally. More information about this collective process and establishing empathy is covered later in the book.

Active Listening is Equally Important

Writing an email, sending a text message, or giving instructions or information orally can all be a part of impactful communication. However, if you do not listen or read what other people have to say, you are ignoring more than half of the interaction equation. This is not about making speeches or writing articles or instruction manuals to your audience. Spoken or written dialogue must balance input and output if you want it to matter and to make a difference in the end.

2) Why Good Communication Matters

The most basic answer to this question is because you want people to listen to what you have to say and understand. Good communication makes everything easier because it removes questions, misunderstandings, and doubt. It helps prevent arguments and negative impressions that can lead to noncompliance or poor outcomes for whatever goals exist.

The Practical Problems of No Impact

Quality communication between higher ups and workers and between members of project teams leads to increased efficiency and ultimately earnings. In a business, both verbal and written contact must align with the overall goals of the company. It also must reach the intended targets in a way that makes sense.

Data collected from more than 400 corporations showed an approximate $62 million annual cost associated with misunderstandings and misinformation. Whatever the issues were, they lead to decreased productivity and more mistakes that needed correction. If you have ever been involved with a project team or department that relies on a manager or boss's instructions, you know how difficult things get when they cannot express themselves clearly and failed to share all essential information.

Poor communication creates undesirable outcomes:

- No or limited focus for forward progress
- Misunderstanding of the purpose behind actions
- Limited creative thought or innovation
- Morale destruction
- Decreased credibility and trust

Communicating with impact improves worker engagement, which means every person works harder and smarter within the group. No one likes to bumble about without clear direction and wonder if they are doing their job correctly. This is the type of situation that results from weak communication.

Personal Risks With Poor Communication

If you cannot convey meaning or intention to your employees, coworkers, or any other group, they are not going to respect you very much. In general, people want to do a good job. They take pride in their work or efforts for the benefit of others.

However, if all they get is partial information or communiqué that does not engage them in a positive way, the fallout could be considerable.

A lack of focus and understanding about the other people involved in the conversation leads to negativity and increased challenges in the future. Take a moment to think about team leaders or managers you had in the past. Some may have taken a very standoffish approach and failed to give you sufficient information at all. Others may have been overbearing and tried to force compliance and understanding without any empathy whatsoever. Did you like these people? Did you want to work hard for them?

If the answer is 'no' to either of these questions, just think how people you talk to could change their mind about you. One conversation or message could transform a pleasant, mutually beneficial relationship into ruins. The moment respect or appreciation vanishes, it will be extremely difficult for any future interactions to work.

The term "impact" in the title of this book has nothing to do with force. You are not trying to hammer information or comprehension into other people's heads. Instead, it is about creating an effective bond that leads to positive outcomes both on a professional and personal level.

3) Know Yourself First to Improve Communication

Knowing your audience or the other people involved in a conversation matters so you can connect with them effectively. Before you get to that part of the process, you must know yourself first.

Some essential questions to answer include:

- How does your personality play into your communication style?
- What strengths can you expand to improve impact?
- What weaknesses get in the way of connecting with others?

It is impossible to come up with a short list of tips or tricks that everyone can use to become more impactful. If it were that easy, no one would ever have a problem with communication. You could learn how to project your voice, proper grammar for business emails, or the latest colloquialisms for friendly texts, but they will not create the outcome you want unless you know how you operate first.

The point of improving your skills is to not destroy your existing personality or transform you into some highly effective automaton. People who interact with you on a personal or professional level want to forge a positive relationship. You do not have to become friends with everybody, but you do need to set them at ease and establish at least a baseline of trust. How can your personality contribute to those things?

Identify Your Strengths and Weaknesses

Besides following a checklist of recommended qualities, the best way to figure out your best and worst traits is to collect data and analyze the response you get. How do people respond to your contact and conversations?

Consider the following examples:

Bob leads a team working on a new software application. He chats with every member of the team every day, asks about how they're feeling, what they're having for lunch, and whether they think they're part of the project is going smoothly. Everyone likes Bob. He's a friendly guy who gives the impression that everyone is doing a great job. However, when the deadline comes for the project, many workers find that they did not finish to the desired specifications. The big boss gets angry, Bob gets in trouble, and feels hurt that his team didn't deliver. In turn, the group feels let down and loses trust in their leader.

Bob has strong personal communication skills. He's great at developing positive working relationships and making sure everybody gets along. Bob has weak professional communication skills. Failed to convey precise information needed to reach a shared goal.

Mary is all about technical precision. When she leads a team, she makes sure everyone knows their job and gets it done on time. She organizes frequent group meetings in which she lists data points about progress and harangues everyone to speed up and work harder. When the deadline arrives, individual parts of the project are complete but the overall thing lacks cohesiveness and team members struggle to fit things together properly. They feel let down by Mary's overbearing leadership that did not encourage questions, concerns, or cross-communication everyone could take part in.

Mary's communication focuses on facts instead of people. Since she fails to take the others' personalities into account, she is more of a human to-do list with built-in accountability than a leader. The team members don't like Mary and are much less likely to work well for her in the future.

Both of them failed to recognize their own strengths and weaknesses before taking on tasks that needed strong verbal and written interaction throughout. Unfortunately, figuring out these things for yourself presents a challenge. If possible, ask the people around you for feedback.

4) Main Barriers to Quality Communication

Many things can block communication on all sides. Of course, you cannot change how other people act or think in any intrinsic way. You need to focus on overcoming your own weaknesses in order to create a better end result for everyone. Unless you have multiple sources of feedback, you may struggle to figure out what is getting in the way of creating a true impact.

Clues your message is not getting through:

- Glazed eyes, no expression, distraction, and general disinterest

- People asking for the same information you already covered
- Questions about things not related to your message
- Frustration or fear about lack of understanding
- Avoidance. People go out of their way to talk to or message someone else

If any of these things happen on a regular basis, too many barriers exist that you are not finding a way around. Identifying that a problem exists is one thing. Understanding why it exists is another. All of these problems happen for specific reasons. These barriers to quality communication are concrete things you can learn to overcome or eradicate.

Language Differences, Technical Terms, and Jargon

In today's interconnected world, almost every business operates on a global scale with people from different countries and cultures. The Internet allows you to socialize with people anywhere on Earth.

Language differences get in the way. This extends from gross misunderstandings to subtle connotations found in idioms, common metaphors, and colloquial expressions.

Even if all the people involved in a conversation or message group speak the same language, overly technical jargon or industry-specific abbreviations can present a huge barrier. Unless only interacting with a small group of people with the same expertise, plain language works better.

Physical or Functional Difficulties

Physical barriers include hearing disorders, reading comprehension weaknesses, and cognitive issues with focus and memory. Functional barriers get in the way of communication transmission. Someone's phone broke, their email server glitches, or the paper left on their desk blew off when the door opened. These issues either have no real solutions or the individual is responsible for overcoming them personally.

Expectations, Bias, and Emotional Barriers

Both sides of any conversation involve expectations and preconceived notions that you may not recognize or understand. Of course, serious issues like racism block impactful communication. Even the most accepting and congenial person judges others based on experience and preconception, however. A listener may expect a speaker to say something because it always happened that way in the past.

Emotional barriers are difficult to regulate and overcome. While some have social anxiety issues that make communication difficult, others fear interactions because of unexpected or unwanted outcomes. Without the skills to make the proper impact, everyone involved gets uncomfortable. A Harris Poll survey of several hundred business managers revealed that a full 69% of them were uncomfortable with "communicating in general. »

Introverts and extroverts view communication quite differently, too. Everything from a casual chat to a corporate meeting involves an exchange of mental and emotional energy. Familiarize yourself with different approaches to the same messages to offer flexible contact styles to different types of people.

Disinterest, Irrelevance, and Boredom

If you say the right thing to the wrong audience, no one will care to pay attention. One of the largest barriers to clear communication is irrelevance. Luckily, it is also one of the easiest to overcome. Do not waste your effort sharing information or interacting with an audience that receives no benefit from what you say. This not only affects impact in the short term but will also destroy their desire to listen to you ever again.

Of course, effective interaction depends on more than speaking clearly to the right audience. Active listening and engagement are essential parts of creating the right type of impact for everyone involved.

Clues you are not listening like you should:

- Attempts to bring the conversation back to your original idea
- Interrupting others or responding to quickly too messages
- You jump to conclusions based on your own expectations or bias
- Sharing information rather than answering questions

5) Keys to Better Communication

Although the whole subject of improving communication skills includes numerous facets and details, there are several key ways to get better. These represent the building blocks of interacting in an impactful way that benefits not only everyone involved but the bigger picture. That could mean the project team you are all working in, the company or organization, or simply a networking group striving toward a common goal.

Recognize Significance

Before you speak, write an email, or send a text message, figure out significance of your words and ideas. Why are you sending this information to those specific people? Does it have an important impact on their work or life?

Taking a moment to examine the significance of every communication before you begin will cut down on wasted effort, misunderstanding, and the chance of boring people with things they do not care about.

Substance Without Fluff

If your words matter, get to the point quickly and clearly. Share only what is necessary to get your point across in a pleasant manner and leave out excess fluff that could diminish your message. The moment you start to ramble or go off on tangents is the moment your communication loses efficacy. Also, people with language or functional barriers will find it much more difficult to understand your point.

Share With Clarity and Intention

Make sure your goals and intentions come through clearly in your message or speech. Everything you communicate to someone else has a reason behind it. What do you want to happen? What do you want them to do with it? This will encourage more interaction and sharing of ideas.

Use Accessible Language and Methods

Skip the jargon and highly technical language unless the terms are necessary for the purpose at hand. Of course, if you are sharing tech specifications for an engineering project, you cannot get away with simple English. For more general topics, use clear and precise language that everyone can understand.

Also, send information using the best methods possible for the recipients. If most of your team prefers text messages, use them. Do not have a face-to-face meeting unless there is a good reason for it. Avoid communication methods that cause frustration or wasted time.

Present a Positive and Inviting Tone

Even the most technical or professional conversation should include a level of positive personal interaction. You do not have to be best friends with your coworkers, but maintaining positive morale matters if you all have to work together to reach your goals. A large part of this involves making sure others know that you are open to responses, questions, and feedback.

Encourage Questions and Feedback

When you come out and clearly state you are available to answer questions and respond to comments, the people you communicate with feel more engaged with the process. Everyone also feels more valued and appreciated. Always remember that good listening skills (or reading messages and responding skills) are essential to communicating with impact over multiple interactions.

Listen and Engage With the Process

Give examples, ask for clarification, encourage new ideas, and welcome creativity any time you communicate with others. Not only can these things boost the overall efficacy of any interaction, they can also bring about interesting and beneficial changes for everyone involved. After all, the end goal of business communication is to improve efficiency, raise morale, and ultimately help the company succeed. This requires everyone to engage effectively with each other.

6) Different Communication Style Explained

Experts identify five different communication styles that people use in different situations and when interacting with a variety of people. Each comes with positive and negative characteristics that affect how others view you and how impactful your communication is. Identify the ones you use most frequently and recognize how to transform your style into something more effective.

Passive Style

This style almost lacks communication at all. Passive people readily go along with the majority, do not speak up often, and take a very laid-back approach to interactions.

Pros – Not likely to make waves, nonconfrontational, easy to get along with. *Cons* – Negativity builds up, misunderstandings happen, they do not feel understood or included.

When a team debates whether they should go with program A or system B, the passive communicator may simply say, "I don't mind either. We can to whatever everyone else wants to."

Submissive Style

Some group submissive communicators with passive ones, but a subtle difference exists. They not only failed to assert their own ideas, but they also truly believe that others are more important and valid.

Pros – Nonconfrontational, may soothe more aggressive people's feelings.
Cons – Ineffectual in a team and does not contribute much to any interaction.

In a conversation about assigning tasks to a group, the submissive communicator will yield to everyone else's choices even if they conflict with their own hidden ideas.

Aggressive Style

People who communicate aggressively are loud, overbearing, intimidating, and forceful when it comes to asserting their own power over a group.

Pros – They get things done and can make powerful leaders.

Cons – No one likes them much, and they can easily bring down the morale of any group.

Any conversation becomes a power struggle with an aggressive person insisting they are right and should get their own way regardless of anyone else's input or objections. If something goes wrong, they are very quick to point fingers and place blame. Eventually, no one else wants to speak up or send a message because they fear retaliation or criticism.

Passive-Aggressive

This odd combination frequently comes across as sarcasm or cynicism. On the surface, they may appear compliant and accepting of the major points of any communication. Underneath, however, they harbor resentment and disagreement that will indubitably erupt at a later time.

Pros – There really are no advantages to passive-aggressive communication.

Cons – Continuous undermining of progress, negative personal interactions, and resentment.

When someone makes a suggestion in the group that the passive-aggressive person does not like, they are likely to roll their eyes and say something like, "Well, I don't mind, but I highly doubt anyone else would go along with such a suggestion." They make sure people get their underhanded remarks while maintaining a façade of agreement.

Assertive Style

Combine the fervor of aggressive communicators with a pleasant demeanor, positive intentions, and good listening skills, and you have an assertive person who offers a lot to any group. These people freely express themselves and share opinions and ideas but also take everyone else's into account.

Pros – Everyone wins in an interaction. Free exchange of ideas is encouraged.

Cons – If they are not the de facto leader of a group, they may quickly become so due to their powerful communication skills.

In the middle of a project meeting with passive communicator stepping back, aggressive ones trying to insist their way is the only way, and passive-aggressive members scoffing and muttering, the assertive person speaks up and says, "I am happy to consider all your opinions. We all deserve an equal chance to make our cases known."

No matter what type of communicators you interact with on a regular basis, you still have to find a way to make the right type of impact. Besides understanding yourself and any potential barriers to clear expression on your side, you must also know how others receive messages from you. This goes a long way to ensure everyone understands and is encouraged to take appropriate action.

B - Reinforce the Impact of Your Messages

If you send a message to someone either verbally or through the written word and they do not understand it or receive the information, is it any better than if you had never shared it to begin with? This extended version of the classic philosophical query, "If a tree falls in the forest and there is no one around to hear it, does it make a sound?" focuses on reception is the most important part of the communication process.

When you learn to speak clearly or craft a text message, you have only achieved half of your impact goals. In order to reinforce them, your delivery must focus on how others receive messages. You want to make an impression that means something. You can only do this if the recipients do something with your message. This could include answering a question, providing feedback, taking a desired action, or simply changing their ideas.

1) Understand How Others Receive Messages

As important as formulating a meaningful message is, some people may still not receive it in a way that makes sense to them. You could argue that their listening skills are outside of your control. In some ways, this is true. However, you still need to get your message across. In most circumstances, you cannot risk misunderstandings or complete breakdown of the process.

You need to transfer information from your own mind to someone else's through oral or written language. Things like body language and graphic depictions of data also affect things. If the person can hear or read, you may imagine that they will receive that information without much trouble. Even if they cannot, you could still transfer information with a chart, map, or diagram. However, so many different factors go into the process, and each one can cause some type of block that stops the transfer of whatever you are trying to convey.

The communication process involves three main steps:

- Encoding the message (talking, writing, body language, graphics)
- Transferring the message (oral speech, written documents, digital transfer)
- Decoding the message (hearing, reading, viewing)

The person who wants to share the information needs to encode it in a way they know their audience will understand. The audience is responsible for decoding it and watching the process over again by giving feedback or some type of response.

2) How to Send a Universally Understood Message

Is it possible to say or write one thing that everyone can understand in the same way?

Individuals come to an interaction with different experiences, biases, learning styles, and listening skills. Innumerable factors exist that influence how they understand anything from technical instructions to casual opinions. With this type of diversity, it may seem that sending universally understood messages is an impossible task.

Unfortunately, that assumption is technically correct. You will never reach every single person with the same message in the same way. However, because most communication focuses on a specific group with shared characteristics who come together for a unique purpose, "universal" is not as far-reaching as it seems.

Whether you are giving an interactive class to hundreds at a large convention or working with a small group project team, the people are there because they want to hear or read what you have to share. Making those things understandable for the specific audience is easier because your goals already align with their interests.

Why Universal Understanding Matters

A large part of quality communication involves tailoring messages to the people involved in the conversation or your audience. However, you cannot come up with a dozen versions of the same speech or text and deliver them to specific groups separately. The ability to craft a universally understood message saves time, energy, and allows everyone to get on the same page.

How to Encourage Understanding for All

Know your goal and make sure it aligns with your communication partner's goals. Share in the most accessible formats using language everyone understands. Stress the most important parts with dramatic emphasis or written tricks like bold or italicized text. Repeat essential information to help people remember. Finally, take regular breaks to check understanding so everyone keeps up at the same pace.

Consider the following example: Project leader Raul is responsible for development, design, and sales teams for a new mechanical engineering device. Meeting with everyone separately makes sense to talk about specific and technical parts of their responsibilities. However, he encourages whole-team integration so everyone stays on track and on deadline.

Instead of using these larger meetings to talk tech to the developers, creatively brainstorm with the design team, and discuss ROI and marketing with the sales experts, he uses natural and understandable language to bridge gaps between the groups. The end goal is the same: to deliver a working machine to the client on budget and on time. Since everyone there shares that goal, Raul focuses all communication on it.

The programmers understand the physical specifications that they must work with. The CAD experts stay on track with costs. The sales and marketing groups can identify development and design features that will make their job simpler when it comes time to present the finished product to potential clients.

Clarity, simple language, and interaction fuel universal understanding even when the people involved look at things in a different way. What truly makes for an expert communicator, however, is the ability to tweak methods and styles to suit a particular audience.

What You Say Is Not the Only Thing That Matters

HOW you say something affects the impact of your message even more. The earlier explanation of passive, submissive, aggressive, and assertive communicators shows how different emotional or behavioral habits affect everything. All these different people can say the same exact thing and yet have a very different outcome.

Many things affect impact you make beyond psychological categories. You can train yourself to speak and write in ways that improve understanding and meaning for everyone. At the same time, you make whatever you have to say or write more interesting and memorable.

3) Reinforce Impact Through Voice Modulation

No one wants to listen to a monotone voice trailing on and on without pauses or changes in inflection. Most listeners will either fall asleep or start to daydream after a very short amount of time. A dull drone makes no impact at all.

On the other hand, excessively animated voices may make people tune out, too. If you accentuate the wrong words or phrases, pause in uncomfortable places, or fail to use emotive voice modulation correctly, you will lose your audience just as easily. You may either end up annoying people or sounding like the proverbial used car salesman going on as if every statement deserves three exclamation points.

Use Voice Modulation Wisely

First, understand that voice modulation is the ability to control the volume and tone of everything you say. For example, if you growl "Look out for ducks" in a deep, slow voice, people will imagine a flock of bloodthirsty fowl ready to attack. If you say the same sentence in a louder, higher pitched voice, it sounds more like an invitation to check out the lovely birds at a community lake.

Tone conveys mood. Volume indicates importance. Both these things can effectively reengage people whose attention has started to drift.

General tips for appropriate voice modulation include:

- Always speak loudly enough that everyone can hear you, but do not shout.
- Speak louder when you want to get attention on a particular word or phrase.

- Speak softer to encourage intense focus.
- Smile when you speak to uplift the tone of your words.
- Pay attention to the speed and rhythm of your sentences and questions.
- Use pauses between important points and different topics.
- A pause sounds better than an umm or ahh.
- Use an enthusiastic tone when asking for questions or comments.

Although it is difficult to give vocal examples in a book, consider how these sentences would sound read out loud.

1 – Do not **CALL** yourself a… umm… leader unless you know the best direction to **TAKE**. Followers **NEED** to trust… ahh… you before they take the first **STEP**.

In this example, the speaker emphasized the wrong words. "Call" and "take" are not the main points the audience should pay attention to. The umm and ahh interrupt flow and take away from overall impact.

2 – Do not call yourself a leader unless you know the **BEST** direction to take. (Pause) Followers need to **TRUST** you before they take the first step.

This makes more impact because it focuses on the best direction and trust, which are much more important to the overall meaning than the emphasized words in the first example. The dramatic pause between the sentences gives the listener time to fully internalize the first idea.

Mood Modulation in Written Communication

When it comes to letters, emails, and texts, using modulation techniques has its own set of issues. It is quite simple to use bold fonts, italics, or different size or color typefaces for emphasis and impact. Of course, you should not go overboard and make your messages look like an elementary school flyer.

Even with these basic text tools, many people struggle to determine the intended tone of a written message. This is especially true for texts because they are short. While it helps to assume good intentions so you do not take offense at a blunt statement, recipients of your messages can still react badly.

This is another instance where you must compensate for unconscious biases and preconceived notions in order to make the most positive impact with your words. Some people would suggest ending every short message with a smiley emoji, but that really does not work in a professional environment. Instead, take a few extra seconds to use words with positive connotations and tone.

People will view the following two text messages very differently:

- Meeting at 2 PM. Prepare for hard questions.
- Meeting at 2 PM. Let's find the best answers together.

With the first example, your team will show up nervous. In the second, they will

be eager to work as a team on solutions
that benefit everyone. It is easy to see
which would be a more productive
meeting.

C - Build a Strong Relationship With an Audience

The matter what the venue or size the group, effective communication requires establishing rapport with the audience. Even if you are giving a speech with no question or comments possible, you still need to form a bond that allows for the smooth transition of your words to their minds.

In work environments, managers and employees or project team members have a built-in relationship already. However, this type of forced connection does little to actually improve how well people communicate with each other. One-time conversations or presentations do not even include this.

The idea of building a relationship like this is very similar to how companies engage consumers with meaningful and impactful marketing messages. In some ways, every conversation is a type of marketing. You share your ideas and opinions with others in hopes that they will understand and accept them. Instead of responding with a purchase, they respond with feedback about what you had to say.

Basic audience relationship building steps include:

- Identifying who your audience is and understanding them.
- Sharing information your audience wants or needs.
- Creating empathy and a more personal bond.
- Interact with questions, active listening, and feedback.
- Pay attention to responses and tweak your communication style to fit.

1) Why a Solid Foundation Relationship Helps

People trust you if you establish a positive relationship with them before you try to convince them of anything. People are more likely to listen to those they know. They stay engaged with conversations for a longer period of time and are more likely to interact to make the communication even stronger.

The importance of building a strong relationship with your audience cannot be understated. Even in the corporate world today, people look for more personal interactions. Everyone wants to feel like they matter and that their thoughts and opinions will be taken into account. This is the type of thing that happens in a respectful relationship. It does not happen in more traditional, standoffish hierarchies where the higher up simply expects others to listen to them without question.

Learning how to build this type of relationship and employing the best methods will elevate your communication skills considerably. However, good communication is also one of the main ways to forge these bonds to begin with. It is a continuous and interactive process.

2) Capture Audience Attention Effectively

Every speech or important conversation must start with an effective hook. The subject of grabbing attention is often compared to fishing at a lake. You use some sort of bait to attract attention and, when the right target comes along, you set the hook and reel them in. Communicating with impact does not involve worms or sharp bits of metal, however.

The Bait – This starts with anything from a piece of marketing material for a lecture to a simple "Hello!" The first word to say must elicit an emotional response. Every attempt at communication must attract your audience in some way. They need of reason to listen to you.

The Hook – This captures their attention and convinces them to stick around. In most cases, it includes the information that they want from the interaction. Let your audience know early on that you are about to provide something valuable to them.

On the Line – Keep your audience engaged throughout the entire speech or conversation to make a true impact. This requires additional valuable information and enough entertainment to keep things interesting.

Catch Their Attention Right Away (The Bait)

Engage your audience's emotions with a surprising sentence or unexpected idea. Use dramatic emphasis effectively while conveying information that promises more. Some possibilities include sharing an unbelievable fact or statistic, asking a rhetorical question, or making a statement that seems nonsensical or purely imaginative.

"Would you take five minutes out of your day to do a simple task to increase ROI by 200%?"

"Less than 20% of people around the world wash their hands after using the bathroom."

Engage Your Audience Effectively (The Hook)

Demonstrate how important whatever you have to say is to your audience. Make it all about them. Talk about potential problems they may have, empathize effectively, and segue into solutions. At this point, keep it relatively simple. This is not the time to lecture, teach, or interact. It is the time to convince them that they want to stick around for the more in-depth discussion later on.

"Every investor has turned you down. Your only options left are personal credit cards or a home equity loan. In the next half hour, I'll give you a step-by-step process to fund your new business venture without risking your family's money."

Captivate Them and Keep Their Attention (On the Line)

Instead of simply quoting statistics or giving a step-by-step plan, make things entertaining with anecdotes and storytelling. Weave examples your audience can relate to into the more technical or idea-driven information. Balance more complicated topics with action and anecdotes to improve comprehension for a wider variety of listeners.

"During college, I worked at the bookshop and a local gas station to pay for my classes. My friend John worked the midnight shift at the grocery store. Creative funding options for advanced education can help prevent this type of overwork and stress so your kids can focus on their studies."

Throughout the whole process of capturing and keeping your audience's attention, use your personality as a springboard for what you say and how you say it. However, if you tend toward laid-back or laconic, you may want to inject a bit more humor or animation into your talk. After all, remember that communication is about serving your audience to make maximum impact.

Consider Multi-Media Presentations and Props

The best communication often goes beyond speaking and writing. Using multimedia presentations, printed material, and props can capture and keep attention effectively. These engage a higher percentage of your audience because people learn and remember things in different ways.

Three rules of using media and props:

Relevancy – Use the right display or object at the right time during your speech for emphasis rather than distraction.

Visibility – Make screens or printed posters large enough for everyone to see them easily. Do not choose props that fit in your hand or need to sit on the table out of line of sight.

Emotional Impact – While hanging a poster of your company logo can boost brand recognition, it does little to augment the power of your words. Only use extras to increase interest and put the focus on specific parts of your presentation.

Another way to incite interest is to encourage audience participation. No, you do not have to invite someone up onto the stage and make them wear a funny hat. Consider handing out printouts or physical objects that reinforce your message. Make sure they are not going to distract them from what you have to say.

This last idea works well in smaller conversations, too. Even if you are having a chat with your neighbor about vegetable gardening, sharing a packet of seeds or a piece of produce increases their investment in the communication. For large-scale corporate events, product samples or promotional items can work well.

3) Passion for the Subject Is the Best Weapon

While you can fabricate effective bait, hooks, and lectures using these tips and creativity, the best way to engage others is to let your natural passion for the subject shine through. It does not make any sense to give a speech or start a conversation about something you do not care about at all. Of course, you sometimes need to do this for your career and still make the communication as engaging as possible.

When your interest level is high, you have an existing stock of anecdotes to share. Your tone of voice, modulation, and emphasis will naturally empower your words. Your passion and excitement will leap from your presentation to the people listening and watching it.

Can you fake interest in a topic if you need to convey information you do not really care about? It is possible, but you do not want to run the risk of your audience recognizing your lack of passion. Plan an effective presentation more fully before you begin because you will not have natural energy to carry you through any part. Be careful not to go overboard with volume, vocal tone, or grand gestures. If you do not have passion, you probably need more practice to make things sound natural and engaging.

4) How Voice Tone and Rhythm Accentuate the Message

Local tone and speaking rhythm contribute to how an audience receives your message. In some ways, public speaking or information exchanges with a group are similar to acting. No, you do not have to pretend to be someone else to get your point across. However, using techniques the professionals practice can help you convey your message in a way that excites other people.

If you are responsible for lectures, presentations, or frequent group leadership roles, you might try a public speaking or acting class to learn these techniques. They will also help build your confidence so your voice sounds natural and anxiety-free while you communicate with the audience.

Vocal Tone Conveys Emotion

The tone of voice you use in conversation or lectures affects the emotional response of your chat partners or audience. The ability to purposefully manipulate your tone gives you a powerful tool to increase interest and impact of whatever information you want to convey. This is something most people have to practice so it sounds natural yet still effective.

People have a very broad repertoire of vocal tones and wordless sounds that express emotion clearly to others. This includes everything from the "Ahh!" of fear to a "Hmm" of deep thought to the "Oh!" of happy surprise. In fact, researchers published in the *American Psychologist* Journal identified 24 different emotions conveyed by the human voice. They even mapped them.

This interesting research does not mean you should interject emotional sounds every time you try to communicate with other people. Your audience may find it odd if you start shouting, "Oh!" and "Ahh!" In the middle of a lecture or group discussion. However, the tonal quality of these sounds teaches you something about modulating your voice.

Emotional Transfer Engages Audiences

Any interaction between two or more people involves a transfer of emotion and thought. Communication is all about getting your ideas and opinions into someone else's brain. Doing the same thing with emotions increases the impact of those ideas. People become more invested in things that make them feel as well as think.

How do you do this without sounding like a melodramatic actor?

For the most part, it all happens naturally. If you are talking about something that excites you, your voice will get louder and higher in tone. If you switch to a subject more serious or sad, your tone drops. Unfortunately, some people have less expressive voices and need to make a conscious effort to change how your voice conveys emotion.

5) Strengthen Audience Bond With Power Words and Gestures

You may think that what you say matters more than anything else when it comes to verbal communication. While the information shared is important, making an impact depends on emphasis. As described earlier in this book, vocal modulation and tone goes a long way to giving your audience hints about the most important parts of whatever you have to say. Another way to do this is with power words.

What Are Power Words?

The term 'power words' seems self-explanatory. These specific words or phrases capture attention, convey more meaning, and create a greater emotional response than ordinary ones. They are not long, complicated, or part of any particular jargon-based vocabulary. They are words anyone can understand. After all, if no one understands what you are saying, they will not get any impact from it.

In marketing, one of the most powerful words is 'free.' When people see this word, they are more likely to take notice of all the written communication around it. People want free stuff. It triggers an emotional response associated with desire.

Many power words focus specifically on emotions, feelings, and sought-after qualities. Terms like inspiring, huge, irresistible, life-changing, simple, guaranteed, and luxurious spark imagination and create positive feelings. Power words that evoke negative feelings your audience wants to avoid also work, such as embarrassing, guilt, mistake, or unpopular. Power verbs inspire people to take action. Some popular ones include kickstart, grow, attack, succeed, and launch.

Point of view also affects the way people respond to your communication. First person, using 'I' and 'we,' creates a sense of camaraderie and togetherness. This can work well for group projects and shared interests. Second person, using 'you,' focuses on individual benefits to your audience. They end up feeling like your message is just for them and that you care about their success. Third person, using 'he,' 'she,' and 'they,' is more formal and less emotionally effective than other options.

Consider these examples for power words and point of view:

Boring and Bland – Everyone wants to make more money. These methods will help people find ways to make income go up. They will feel better when they do not have to worry as much about paying bills.

Powerful and Personal -- You dream about an exceptional lifestyle of luxury and freedom. Learn life-changing ways to explode your income in less time than you expect. Kickstart a brand-new adventure that lets you focus on fun instead of financial worry.

While these examples sound more like marketing blurbs than a conversation, they represent using power words in communication effectively. You can see that the second example has more specific and emotive phrases that will get people's attention and keep it from the first sentence to the last. By contrast, the boring example feels vague and disconnected from the audience.

Nonverbal Communication and Body Language Helps

Physical gestures and body language also provide the type of emphasis that many audiences need to stay connected to the conversation. Various research studies find that body positions and gestures contribute anywhere from 60% to 90% of meaning.

This type of communication begins even before you open your mouth. Of course, it does not matter at all in written communication, so letters, emails, and text messages may need extra power words or emotional language to truly convey meaning with impact.

Three points of body language power exist:

- Body positioning, posture, and stance
- Where you put or move your hands and arms, gestures
- Movement or position of your head

Imagine you walk into a business meeting and your manager slumps over in his chair, elbows on the desk, and head in his hands. He stares down at a folder instead of making eye contact with anyone in the room. How does his posture and positioning affect your emotional response? If you are like most people, you probably get a bit nervous because his body language clearly conveys negative feelings.

If you walk into the same business meeting and find your manager up on his feet, smiling at each participant as they walk in the room, and moving in an active yet comfortable way, you would naturally feel more positive about the meeting.

Of course, there are always extenuating circumstances. Maybe in the first example, your manager had a twisted ankle and a headache from his allergies. He may feel rundown, but it had nothing to do with the content of the meeting. Hopefully, he could convey a more positive mood and his words and tone of voice.

Managing how other people respond to your communication with positive body language is an effective way of increasing the impact and retention of what you have to say. When you converse with one person, face them with an open and welcoming stance. Use good posture for a more positive impression. Mirror body language to increase comfort levels. Stay relaxed and gesture effectively without making people fear standing too close.

Specific tips for large-scale presentations:

- Stand up or walk about the stage to face all sections of the audience.
- Do not lean excessively on a table or podium like you are tired.
- Do not cross your arms as this looks aggressive or angry.
- Gesture toward multimedia presentations or while using props.
- Avoid excessively dramatic movements or gestures.

To clarify the last point, running and leaping across the stage excitedly or waving your arms around may make people take notice, but the emotional response would probably be laughter and loss of respect rather than anything positive. Even if you feel excited or passionate about the subject, grandiose gestures cross the line from effective communication to sideshow barker territory.

Facial Expressions Matter Too

Although the finer characteristics of facial expressions may not convey clearly in a large lecture hall, they do contribute to the exchange of emotion present in all communication. People are more likely to take notice of and remember expressions that reveal high levels of emotion rather than face is at rest.

The human brain is wired to make sense out of visual cues that may not mean much on their own. When it comes to facial expressions, these include eye outline, shape and specifically width of the mouth, and symmetry.

Again, making extreme facial expressions while you converse with others or give a lecture is not a way to engage your audience and make an impact. Subtlety communicates just as well. However, it is important not to stand there with a blank face because other people will have a hard time figuring out how you feel and what is most important to pay attention to.

Your voice also sounds different whether you smile or frown. Telemarketers and other people who speak on the phone for business purposes frequently are trained to smile while they read their script or answer questions. It conveys a friendly tone even without any visual cues.

D - Resolve Conflicts Through Communication

Communication is about so much more than sharing ideas or opinions. Sometimes what you share demands a response such as feedback or an answer to a question. When two or more people interact, a chance for conflict always exists. Whether it involves a simple difference in opinion or a downright argument, you need to use your communication skills effectively to solve the problem and bring things back to a more positive place.

Conflict happens for only a few actual reasons:

- Misunderstanding and miscommunication
- Stress, fatigue, frustration, and burnout
- Interpersonal problems between individuals

Misunderstandings and Miscommunication

These are both the most common reasons for conflict and disease simplest to solve through better communication methods. If someone misunderstands your goals or intentions, they may not feel bold enough to ask for clarification. People assume things based on their own experiences and knowledge, but their impressions may not align with your meaning. By the time anyone realizes a miscommunication happened, things may have progressed in the wrong direction for too long.

This leads to frustration and burnout as described below. The only way to prevent these types of conflicts is to express yourself clearly and make sure everyone understands you from the start. Ask for feedback and give the opportunity to ask questions frequently throughout the communication process. Also, keep a record of comments, questions, and answers, so everyone can look back and get the reminder of things they may forget.

Stress, Fatigue, Frustration, and Burnout

People get cranky when they are tired. Unrelenting stress contributes to negative emotions. Burnout happens to everyone eventually. These are serious problems that affect many groups and can transform positive forward motion into conflict and blockages very quickly. Of course, people have their own stresses and difficulties in their personal life that you have no way of knowing about or compensating for. Instead, focus on these issues as they relate to your collaboration.

All communication can re-motivate people or help them recognize new ways forward to prevent additional stress, you cannot talk someone out of fatigue or extend a worrying deadline with a friendly chat. First, identify the source of the stress and frustration and focus on it in a new way. Then, use the most understanding, empathetic, and positive language and voice methods possible to nudge the negativity in a better direction.

Interpersonal Problems Between Individuals

Some people simply do not mesh well. You cannot change the personality of anyone in your group. Nor can you always remove a person from a group or conversation who does not fit in smoothly with the others. Although you can hope that personal issues do not affect a business relationship or professional project, that is unrealistic. Conflicts will happen, and you will have to find a way to deal with them effectively for the benefit of everyone involved.

When possible, prevention works better than trying to fix personal problems after the fact. Select team members carefully and only involve people in a conversation that you think will work smoothly together. This does not mean all project teams should consist of friend groups. If you are in charge of multiple employees, pay attention to how they get along on an everyday basis.

If you cannot prevent problems before they happen, use quality communication techniques to defuse situations and improve understanding and collaboration. Re-create what you say and how you say it if you find your initial communication style or group management techniques do not work. Flexibility matters in these types of situations.

1) Create a Common Reality and Connection

Fairness and equality go a long way to minimizing the risk of conflict in a group. When everyone is treated the same and feels part of a collective team, they are more likely to treat others with respect and work hard for mutual benefit. These general ideas make collective effort better. A large part of creating this kind of situation comes from effective communication.

Everyone Exists in a Common Reality

No matter how diverse the specific demographics or purposes of your team members, they all exist as an integral part of the group. Creating that reality that everyone understands and feels comfortable with depends on communicating what it means to everyone and every individual.

Establishing this type of collective foundation requires introducing it early on and making sure everyone is on board with the same ideas. In general, people want to share connections, feelings, and understanding of the world around them. Some say that humans are pack animals that rely on socialization for a large part of our comfort and purpose. Perception of a bond or shared reality leads to motivation and productivity.
You can use these ideas to create a positive experience for everyone.

The feeling that "We're all in this together" improves interpersonal relations in social and professional settings. How do you make this happen?
1 – Establish boundaries, factual realities, expectations, and goals at the start. In a group setting, communicate everything

possible about the reality you want to create with the group. Leave plenty of time for questions and clarification. If you lay this firm foundation, you have already taken a bold step toward staving off potential conflict down the road.

2 – Invite everyone to share information, ideas, and opinions about everything from project progress to the other people on the team. In order to do this positively, guide the conversation toward increased inclusion by making statements that already align with what others believe or asking questions people already know the answers to. When two or more people share the same information or opinion, it helps others recognize the value of what they communicate.

3 – Create a web of interconnectivity between individuals to reinforce common reality ideas. Make sure to disallow the formation of cliques or pairs that exclude others. Ideally, multi-directional communication should reinforce commonly known concepts instead of segregating them for specific people.

Less conflict happens when everyone feels like an integral part of the whole. Facilitating connections that include rather than exclude makes it easier for people to talk about issues rather than taking sides. The moment when winning and losing becomes the focus, communication has broken down completely, and you may find it very difficult to regain movement in a positive direction for everyone.

2) Regulate Tension with the DESC / DEAR Methods

Although they use different acronyms, the DESC and DEAR methods of managing difficult communication follow the same basic principles and practices. These are associated with active listening and responding in a way that defuses conflict, decreases automatic defensiveness, and asserts control over the conversation so it can return to a positive path.

DESC -- Describe, Express, Specify, Consequences

This is not only a great technique to use when communicating with other people, but also an excellent thing to teach people you must work with on a regular basis. It can help transform passive or submissive communicators into assertive ones who stand up for their personal rights.

This structured response focuses on appropriate and honest language that balances emotional response with consideration for others. No one in a professional, adult setting should feel the need to cry out, "You're hurting my feelings!" However, they should also not feel the need to stifle them in the face of suggestions or opinions made by other people.

Use the DESC method to defuse high-tension situations and move toward a productive solution to whatever the problem was in the first place. Works for almost any circumstances and with any number of people involved.

Describe – Clearly state what the problem is or what situation led to the conflict.

Express – Reveal your feelings about the situation without accusations or judgments. Use "I" statements instead of "you" statements that are more likely to cause a defensive response.

Specify – What do you want to happen next? Share preferences for further action toward goals.

Consequences – Not all consequences to conflict are bad. Clearly communicate what the advantages and disadvantages of taking the preferential action you specified.

Consider the following example of a project team whose communication has broken down:

Ava is working on a graphic design project with four coworkers. She needed a series of three samples from Gary on specific dates to stay on the established timeline. He did not deliver. Instead of Ava storming into Gary's office and demanding he get busy and stop messing up the whole project for everyone, she can use the DESC method to improve the outcome with impactful communication.

"Gary, I cannot do my part of the project without the design samples from you." (Describe)
"It makes me nervous that I will not be able to deliver on time." (Express)
"I would like to set up a collaboration meeting so we can finalize the designs together." (Specify)
"If we do that, we can speed up productivity, avoid the need for back-and-forth changes, and meet the deadline with no problems." (Consequences)

With these types of positive statements, Gary is much less likely to respond with anger or defensiveness. He would not feel attacked. Instead, Ava suggests a process that can help him feel more comfortable with getting the work done on time, too. He may have felt overwhelmed or had stressful personal issues getting in the way of his own progress.

DEAR -- Describe, Emotion, Ask, Reiterate

Although similar to the DESC method, this communication tool has a few extra parts frequently added to it. In fact, some experts lengthen the acronym to DEAR MAN.

The letters used for this conflict management tool stand for:

- Describe
- Express
- Assert
- Reinforce
- Mindfulness
- Appear confident
- Negotiate

The first four match the definitions for DESC. The last three add something new that focuses more on staying focused and communicating in a way that gets you what you want in the end. Of course, what you want should be a mutually beneficial solution to the problem you are having with the other person.

Mindfulness – Stick to the topic at hand and do not let yourself get distracted by tangents. When you present a conflict to another person, even if you use the most positive communication methods possible, they may attempt to deflect bringing up something else. It could be a conscious choice to take the heat off or a sincere expression of their own issues. Following the new comment down a rabbit hole does nothing to solve the problem at hand. Stay mindful of the current situation so you can work together to make it better before moving on to something else.

Appear Confident – Even while expressing negative emotions about the conflict, use confident postures, words, and behaviors to give the other person the impression that what you have to say is important and viable for the situation. Confidence also helps you avoid arguments because your statements do not invite them. Discussion, yes. Additional conflict, no.

Negotiate – The goal of positive communication is to solve conflicts in the best way for everyone involved. This is not about you getting your way and making everyone give up what they want in the process. Whoever else is involved in the conversation should have equal opportunity to express their own feelings and interests in the matter. Negotiation is all about compromise, which means both parties benefit to some degree.

3) How to Express Challenges Constructively

A large part of the aforementioned communication methods involves expressing conflicts or challenges in a way acceptable to everyone involved. You do not want to trigger a negative emotional response that leads to defensiveness, passive-aggressive behavior, or outright rejection. Whether you are speaking with an individual or a large group, there are ways to talk about problems that bypass the chance of making everything worse.

Stick to the Facts of the Situation

Accept reality for what it is and look at the situation objectively. This should happen before you start communicating about solutions or a plan to find one. However, it does help to talk with others to get their opinion about what the facts are. Many challenges and conflicts occur due to misunderstandings or different perspectives. Once you separate fact from opinions, you have a firm foundation to begin the next stage of the process.

When you express the challenge to other people, communicate with as much objective truth as possible. Be aware of your own biases and experiences that may taint your explanations.

Never Point Fingers or Place Blame

In a conversation or communiqué about a challenge, it does not matter if one person worked to slowly or another rejected all workable options. Placing blame or pointing fingers at other people involved in the situation does not lead toward conflict resolution. Remain calm and neutral when you speak with others. This is not a time to confront poor work ethic or rule breaking. That is a matter for individual discussions focused on employment and not the group project.

Do Not Make It All About You

You are not the most important person to please when it comes to challenges at work, within a volunteer organization, or in your personal life. Detach yourself from the outcome by pointing out external factors that matter more. For example, a project team at work must align their efforts with the client's needs. There is always someone or something disconnected from the conflict to focus on.

Stop Overanalyzing Why Challenge Happened

The more you think about why something happened, who caused it, or how it all went down in the first place, the more attention you give to the problem instead of the solution. Challenges happen all the time, and appropriate communication skills can either get you bogged down in conflict or let you rise above to find a better way forward. Over-analyzation leads to increased frustration and stress for everyone involved. People end up feeling like they are under the microscope, which may translate into not getting involved at all. You do not want to create passive or submissive communicators through excessive investigation.

Focus on Change as a Positive Thing

The ancient Greek philosopher Heraclitus said that, "The only constant in life is change." Regardless of this pithy statement that supports the idea of a dynamic reality, many people fear change and see it as a negative thing. This is especially true in a professional situation where changes can lead to confusion, increased stress, a heavier workload, or even layoffs.

When you communicate specifically about a challenge or conflict, remind people that change can lead to great things. Even when these changes push people outside their comfort zone, the results and eventual outcome may be better than expected. Also, clearly express that the process of making a change is not permanent. A new status quo will allow people to be comfortable once more.

No matter what type of challenge or conflict that exists, communication is the key to establishing a shared reality and managing emotional responses to come out the other side in a more positive way. While objectivity and resisting over-analyzation make the most sense, they are not as easy as it sounds.

People are emotional creatures, and a host of experiences and unconscious biases exist that taint all understanding and thought. If you are responsible for communicating throughout these circumstances, the most important thing to have is empathy. More than anything else, this helps you forge connections with individuals and groups in ways that allow for more constructive back and forth dialogue and impactful communication.

E - Know How to Communicate With Empathy

If communication was only an exchange of information, the world would have a lot fewer arguments and conflicts. Instead, emotions get wrapped up in every message on both sides. Trying to weed out feelings from communication is almost impossible. You cannot, after all, force people to feel a certain way for your convenience.

What you can do is practice empathy for everyone involved with the communication experience. This type of understanding will always lead to a better outcome because you can tailor your words, expressions, and gestures to your target audience's state of mind.

1) What Is Empathy?

The basic definition of empathy is the ability to put yourself in another person's shoes and understand where they come from and what they are going through. When it comes to leadership or business relationships, empathy is one of the most appreciated soft skills. It is an essential part of effective communication, too.

In the real world, empathy does not make you feel exactly the same physical or emotional things as another person. However, emotional transference can happen. For example, if your coworker is exceptionally sad because they lost a loved one, empathizing with them means you understand their pain and feel some measure of it on their behalf. It does not mean you enter the grief process the same way they would.

Is Empathy a Learnable Skill?

Some believe that a person is either born with empathy or they cannot develop it no matter how hard they try. The human brain seems hardwired to make emotional connections to things like facial expressions and tones of voice, which change when a person expresses their own feelings. Brain scans actually showed one person's pain receptors triggering when another person experienced pain. This physiological response does not happen with everyone, especially when cognitive biases exist.

In other words, if an individual does not feel a connection to another person, they are much less likely to attempt to empathize with them. Unfortunately, this type of thing happens frequently with different ethnic or religious groups, genders, socioeconomic classes, and due to other perceived differences. Despite these challenges, that does not mean you cannot get better at expressing empathy through communication and encouraging others to do the same.

What Does Empathizing Do?

The stronger connection between coworkers, team members, or people involved in simple dialogue, the more likely they are to work toward a common goal and listen to each other when conflicts arise. The ability to put yourself into someone else's shoes allows you to consider different viewpoints more objectively.

Empathy helps a lot in personal relationships and business activities like sales and customer service, as well. It is the foundation of expressed understanding that puts people on the same level. It naturally creates a sense of camaraderie and teamwork that can translate into greater success for all.

How to Build Empathy For Others

Empathizing with others provides limited benefits if stays inside your own mind and does not affect how you interact with others or approach communication opportunities. However, the work you put in to build empathy has to take place before you open your mouth or start a new email addressing the problem or making suggestions.

These tips will help you establish empathy so you can use it to communicate more constructively:

- Practice looking at problems from other people's perspectives.
- Ask for feedback from groups and individuals including information about why they feel or think the way they do.
- Validate thoughts and feelings by putting them into your own words without changing them to suit your perspective.
- Always practice active listening so you fully understand where the other person is coming from. Ask questions as needed.
- Pay attention to conscious or unconscious biases that taint your opinions. Challenge them constantly so you can explore other perspectives with greater understanding.

How to Communicate a Need for Empathy

Not everyone has the same innate amount of empathy, and some people may not recognize its desirable qualities. As an expert communicator, you can help others understand why empathizing provides benefits and minimizes the risk of conflict for everyone.

In some ways, the methods mimic the kind of things parents or kindergarten teachers say to small children. How do you think the other person feels about that? How would you feel if that happened to you?

As an adult learning to communicate with impact, the last thing you want to do is come across as condescending or overbearing to the people you interact with. Instead of basic questions, encourage everyone in a group to share their ideas and issues, then ask others questions that would demonstrate their understanding from a different perspective.

2) Check for Audience Understanding

A large part of quality communication deals with understanding your audience. In order to deliver an effective speech or engage constructively in a conversation, it helps to know who you are talking to or messaging. Even if you do your homework and target what you have to say to an audience as closely as possible, they still may not understand your meaning or intention.

How do you make sure your audience understands you before you move on to a different topic or end the communication completely? You know how important this is. After all, misunderstandings and miscommunication are two of the most common problems that people face in both personal and professional relationships.

Examine Body Language and Facial Expressions

Nonverbal communication tells you more sometimes than the words people choose. This is especially true if you are making a presentation to a large group where you cannot focus on individuals or ask questions directly.

When you are standing on stage or behind the podium, scanned the crowd for continuity of reaction. Our most of the people looking up at you and seemingly engaged with what you have to say? You cannot hope to grab everyone's attention, so some people will have their faces down looking at their phone or focus elsewhere. The people watching and listening intently demonstrate their understanding. People who are confused or completely lost will stop paying attention rather quickly.

Are most of the people responding with emotional cues at the right places? If you tell a joke or share an entertaining anecdote, most people in the audience should smile. This also demonstrates understanding. Of course, it might only show that they understand your joke and not the content of your lecture.

Large groups and communication at a distance make it harder for you to know if your audience really gets what you are trying to say. If possible, make time for a question-and-answer period after your presentation. This is one of the better ways to check for understanding in any size group.

Take Note of the Questions They Ask

What questions do people ask when they understand what you already said or wrote to them but want more information or increased clarity?

If someone asks a question about something you already explained in full, it shows that what you said did not have the impact you intended. It is possible that individual simply got distracted for a moment, but you cannot dismiss repetitive questions or requests for explanations so easily.

If anyone inquires about topics only tangentially related to your communication or things that have no correlation at all, they either misunderstood your meaning or have a personal agenda to explore. The first demonstrates a complete breakdown in your communication impact. The latter is something you can usually ignore as it would not be your responsibility to address that issue.

In a longer presentation, pause between sections or topics for questions before moving on. This is especially important if later information builds on the understanding of things that came before. You do not want your audience to get lost early on and find the rest of the lecture incomprehensible and useless. In smaller groups engaged in a multi-sided conversation, the same technique works. Welcome questions or even interruptions to ask for clarity or more detail.

Ask for Feedback Directly

Chances are, you will not need to communicate with an individual or group only one time. In order to improve the rate of audience understanding, ask them for feedback about your presentation or the team discussion. A simple, "How did everyone feel about this lecture/discussion today? Was there anything you did not understand? How would you change the communication to be more effective for you personally?"

It is impossible to fully engage every single person you ever communicate with. In a lecture hall, you have no idea if the woman sitting in the fourth row is truly passionate about your subject or if he just showed up for the free lunch. In a small team discussion, you cannot always tell if the man from the sales department agrees with everything because he understands the importance of your ideas or if he just wants the meeting to end so he can get home to his sick child.

All you can do is analyze reactions and ask for feedback directly and communicate using all the skills at your disposal. Learning and improving is a continuous process that will help you create messages that truly have an impact on others.

These things matter a lot in face-to-face communication. However, due to the increase in working at home and international collaborations, communicating well at a distance has become even more important than it ever was before. When you cannot see the people involved in a conversation, it cuts down on your ability to judge audience understanding and use that all-important body language, facial expressions, and vocal tonality to streamline your efforts for greatest impact.

F - Communicate Well at a Distance

Companies and organizations who allow employees to work at home or employ a global workforce have unique communication challenges not found in places where everyone goes to the same building every day. Modern technology has boosted connectivity to a point where instantaneous messaging and virtual meetings are commonplace. However, they do not work for every situation, and they cannot provide the same level of understanding as in-person conversations.

Despite the many issues that come with using dispersed teams, you need the same level of understanding and collaboration to make everything run smoothly. All the other tips for making an impact still exist. Most of the methods still work well. Additional guidance for communicating well at a distance will help when you need to worry about things like different time zones, language barriers, and cultural expectations.

1) Communication Tips for a Dispersed Team

Virtual meetings or network messages cannot happen organically when the people are involved work in different countries at different times and with different levels of understanding. These tips will help smooth the process for maximum team efficacy and minimal conflict.

Remote Teams Need a Communication Plan in Place

Create a strict schedule for virtual meetings and one-on-one communication between team members and managers. Choose times that work for everyone no matter what time zone they are working from. It is unfair to expect someone to go to a meeting at 10 PM or on a day when they do not usually work except in extreme situations.

Set expectations and allowances for contact frequency and times. If a member of the group needs to ask question, they should do so during regular hours or at least understand they may not get an answer until the next business day commences in the recipient's time zone. His types of rules will stave off potential conflict that may arise when people feel ignored or unappreciated.

Communicate More Using Different Methods

Without bombarding dispersed team members with repetitive information, adopt a practice of over-communicating to foster better understanding and camaraderie. Encourage team participation without managerial oversight, too.

Besides an increase in the number of messages and questions to check for understanding and compliance, use multiple types of contact. For example, a virtual meeting platform is a great option for group chats and regular updates. These can happen every week or month depending on the time sensitivity of the project. Email may work better for people with language differences because they have more time to translate or extract meaning from the longer message.

The end goal is to make sure that everyone involved gets all the information they need in an accessible way. Realize that different countries use different pieces of software or platforms more frequently. This is simply a matter of popularity, which can be overcome by a directive from the main office. As long as everyone can get the same program, it should work well for effective communication.

Encourage Interactivity and Empathy Among a Diverse Team

Unfortunately, some employees or independent contractors may have preconceived notions of people from different countries, ethnicities, or with different cultural practices. Working with people like this is an extreme challenge. However, without blatant conflict that would result in disciplinary action, everyone involved needs to learn how to communicate and collaborate in a productive way.

As a leader, the way you communicate with everyone and encourage interactivity will determine a large part of how the process works. Be cognizant of your own biases and reinvent your opinions as necessary. If you identify friction between team members, use empathy to consider the issue from both sides, even one you do not agree with. The DEAR and DESC methods of regulating tension can help in these situations.

Empathy and interactivity build trust within the team. You need to make everyone know that you expect them to do their tasks on time and that the ability to count on them is an essential part of overall success. This should spread through the employee and contractor group to encourage more hands-off management over time.

Quality communication depends in part on establishing a strong foundation of personal connectivity. It helps everyone to know who they are talking to. In an office setting, you see other team members every day. You know if they drink coffee or tea in the morning, whether they share pictures of their family during breaks, or if they go skydiving on the weekend. Dispersed teams do not automatically have that sense of camaraderie. Although the focus should remain on getting the job done, foster friendlier connections, too. Avoid cheesy team-building exercises, which may seem to personal or awkward for some people. Instead, share little stories or details about your own life and ask other people simple questions about theirs. Something as simple as, "How was your weekend?" can contribute to a more receptive and close-knit group who communicates more easily.

Team bonding activities for a geographically dispersed team include:

- Intranet-style page where people can share work-related ideas and inspiration.

- A "coffee break" chat room to share personal information and have fun.
- Language and culture learning opportunities

2) Take Cultural Norms and Expectations Into Account

In groups with people from all around the globe, language barriers may exist. Your dispersed team undoubtedly operates using one common language, but not everyone is as fluent as everyone else, and some may have strong accents.

In order to combat discomfort or embarrassment and promote increased understanding, always remind people to speak slowly and clearly as much as possible. Avoid colloquialisms, slang, and idioms that do not translate well. Also, establish early on that it is acceptable to ask someone else for clarification to prevent misunderstandings.

Avoid Offense and Potential Legal Issues

If you are responsible for managing the communication between team members and the company itself, educate yourself about the countries and cultures everyone comes from. If necessary, post information on a shared group page to ensure no one accidentally offends anyone else. This is especially important if a certain type of comment skates the edge of legality. Not every country has the same freedom of speech rules.

For the most part, discussing work would not cause these problems anyway. However, the last thing you want to do is make one or more team members feel uncomfortable or nervous about future interactions. Ribald humor, adult language, and references to alcohol or LGBTQ issues may get very different reactions in a diverse audience.

Diverse Teams Have Diverse Ways of Handling Business

It is impossible to list all the unique cultural expectations and practices for every nation in the world. As a team leader, you could research where each member is from and do your best to communicate in a way that matches their expectations. While this is culturally sensitive and empathetic, it might not be practical in a dynamic workplace.

The best way to manage expectations is to clearly communicate how the company expects things to flow and how you intend to manage the team. People who work with an international group should understand the need to make changes to their usual operating procedure in order to fit in.

Potential norms and expectations may involve:

- Speaking tone and content (Straightforward and blunt vs. expressive and loquacious)

- Level of personal interaction (Making friends with coworkers vs. all about business)
- Punctuality and scheduling (Regimented and exact vs. flexibility or early/late expected)
- Work hours (Longer = dedication/ achievement vs. wasteful/ inefficient)
- Presentation and dress (Casual at-home wear vs. corporate attire)
- Names and titles (First name basis vs. Sir/Ma'am vs. friend/dear)

When in doubt, opt for more professional communication. Managing cultural expectations and norms does not mean everyone should wear a business suit to a virtual meeting or call each other by their first names if they are not comfortable doing so. It means you need to effectively communicate in a way that suits everyone's needs. Also, work hard to foster understanding of the differences that may cause conflicts between team members. Being forewarned about potential issues can stop them in their tracks.

3) Choose Appropriate Modes of Communication

Diverse groups do not expect or respond well to the same mode of communication. However, it is impossible to send the same message in five different ways so everyone gets it in their preferred way. Distance communication happens either verbally over the phone or with voice messages, through a video conference or call online, or through emails or text messages. For project teams and organized groups, various software platforms that allow communal conversations also work.

With the ever-increasing proliferation of fastest forms of communication, people expect full-time connection these days. The tech like smart phones that supports this have affected expectations. In the past several years, distance communication has become the preferred method with 93% of workers preferring it over face-to-face meetings.

4) Communicate Effectively at a Distance

Distance communication requires telephone, cellular service, or the Internet. Very few people have landline phones anymore. Instead, any calls are made over mobile networks. However, while calling and leaving voice messages remains an option, many people prefer text-based communication instead. Even in the corporate world, sending texts or using an inter-office group platform is more common than both phone calls and email.

Make Phone Calls Productive and Impactful

Make a plan of attack before you pick up the phone to call anyone. Establish your primary and secondary goals for the conversation and keep a cheat sheet of concepts and questions in front of you. Long, rambling chats are fine for calling your parents on the weekend or talking with your significant other at night.

Impactful communication with a specific purpose needs a different approach.

- Greet the other person and identify yourself.
- Clearly state the purpose for the phone call.
- Address questions and concerns.
- Ensure understanding.

Video Calls and Virtual Conferencing

Distance communication does not get any closer to in-person communication then video calls and conferencing. Although you may be on the other side of the world from the others, you can hear their voice and see their facial expressions almost as if you were in the same room together. This makes virtual communication one of the most powerful and effective for meetings and important conversations.

- Ensure everyone can see and hear everyone else.
- Establish rules about who gets to talk when.

- Introduction to give an overview of the meeting.
- Clear communication of information.
- Questions, comments, and feedback.
- Give instructions for work or future meetings.

Short and Convenient – Text Messages Work

People send more than 22 billion texts every single day, and that number is expected to go up as cellular phone coverage expands to even the most remote places on earth. While many of them are personal chats between friends or family members, a considerable number exist between companies and their consumer base or are inter-office communication. More people open and read texts than they answer phone calls or open emails. This makes them one of the most response-oriented modes of distance communication around.

How do you create impact with a simple one or two-sentence text? You do not have room for expressing much emotion, using interesting power words, sharing anecdotes, or long explanations. Instead, focus on clarity and specifics.

- State your point or ask a question right away.
- Avoid abbreviations, emojis, and text speak.
- Include all pertinent information (links, phone numbers, meeting times, etc.)
- Sign your text messages for clarity.
- Stay available for an immediate response.
- Do not resend a text message too soon.

Tips for Effective Email Communication

Email remains one of the more common communication methods within an office or organization. You can convey a lot more information and ask more questions in this long-form structure when compared with shorter text messages and comments on group collaboration platforms.

When it comes to making the right impact with your email communication, focus on structure, language, and length.

Follow these tips for quality email contact:

1 – Address the emails personally. This means not only to make sure your message gets to the right person, but also that they know they were the intended recipient. 'Dear Bob,' or 'Hello Sharona,' at the top of the message fulfills this need and sounds friendlier.

2 – Share critical information right away. In both professional and personal emails, get to the point as soon as possible. Do you need a coworker to bring a file to you before lunch? Do you want to know if your friend is coming to visit next weekend? Time is precious, and people tend to skim emails for pertinent information and to see if they need to respond.

3 – Keep everything short and simple. Get to the point quickly and stay on point until you sign your name at the bottom. However, do not trade thoroughness for brevity. An email is not a text message. Make sure you get all necessary information in one.

4 – Use good language skills. Do not use text speak or questionable abbreviations. Stick with accepted grammar, punctuation, and spelling.

5 – Do you need a response? Ask for it directly. Do not allow the recipient to feel any confusion or doubt when it comes to sending an answer. However, always keep things polite.

Group or Team Collaboration Platforms

Although not a usual mode of communication outside their specific use, group collaboration platforms offer an effective way to share ideas and updates with multiple people at the same time. A quality program includes real-time notifications and conversation capabilities.

These are specifically tailored for people who already share similar interests or goals. For example, a project team developing a new piece of software can use a collaborative tool to report on their progress, pass finished work to the next person in line, or discuss changes requested by the client.

Whether you want to run an efficient meeting with a diverse team, give an engaging and impactful lecture to a conference hall, or send a quick text message to a close associate, effective communication depends on the same things. Know your audience, tailor your message to their needs and expectations, and focus on clarity and empathy to improve understanding and minimize the risk of conflict.

Conclusion

You do not have to change your whole personality to communicate effectively with anyone. The methods described in this book will help you create true impact with any audience, large or small, well-established or full of perfect strangers. Both spoken and written communication involves so many factors that contribute to both understanding and inspiration. No matter what medium you choose, you need to fully engage others if you want to meet your goals.

Whether you are naturally eloquent or nervous and unsure, the information found here can transform your delivery. Improving your ability to communicate is one of the best ways to push your career forward, make changes that matter in this world, and build true relationships with people eager to join you in success.

Communication is both the simplest and most complex subject to master. The key principles – know your audience, choose the right methods, forge connections, manage emotions, and actively listen – build a firm foundation. The specific tips and methods can reinforce exactly the type of impact you wish to make. With new understanding and tools in your arsenal, you can communicate in ways that can effectively change the world and elevate your place in it.

www.ingramcontent.com/pod-product-compliance
Lightning Source LLC
La Vergne TN
LVHW091721190726
843493LV00001B/403